American As Apple Pie

The Only Homemade Apple Pie Cookbook
You Will Ever Need

BY: Valeria Ray

License Notes

Copyright © 2019 Valeria Ray All Rights Reserved

All rights to the content of this book are reserved by the Author without exception unless permission is given stating otherwise.

The Author have no claims as to the authenticity of the content and the Reader bears all responsibility and risk when following the content. The Author is not liable for any reparations, damages, accidents, injuries or other incidents occurring from the Reader following all or part of this publication.

A Special Reward for Purchasing My Book!

Thank you, cherished reader, for purchasing my book and taking the time to read it. As a special reward for your decision, I would like to offer a gift of free and discounted books directly to your inbox. All you need to do is fill in the box below with your email address and name to start getting amazing offers in the comfort of your own home. You will never miss an offer because a reminder will be sent to you. Never miss a deal and get great deals without having to leave the house! Subscribe now and start saving!

https://valeria-ray.gr8.com

Contents

Delicious Apple Pie Recipes 7

(1) Mom's Apple Pie 8

(2) Cranberry Apple Pie 11

(3) Canadian Apple Pie 14

(4) Easy Apple Pie 17

(6) Caramel Pecan Apple Pie 20

(7) Iron Skillet Apple Pie 24

(8) Mini Apple Pies with Almonds 27

(9) Caramel Apple Pie 30

(10) Dutch Apple Berry Pie 33

(11) Mini Apple Pies 35

(12) Apple Pizza Pie 38

(13) Extra Spicy Apple Pie 41

(14) Upside Down Apple Pecan Pie 44

(15) Sour Cream Apple Pie 47

(16) Apple Sheet Cake 50

(17) Apple Blueberry Pie 54

(18) French Apple Pie with Cream Cheese Topping 57

(19) Blueberry Apple Peach Pie 60

(20) Apple Buttermilk Custard Pie 64

(21) Apple Pockets 68

(22) Autumn Fruit Tart 71

(23) Apple Crumble Pie 74

(24) Apple Berry Pie 76

(25) Delicious Caramel Apple Pie 79

(26) Sugar-Free Apple Pie 82

(27) Glazed Apple Cream Pie 85

(28) Apple Crumb Pie 89

(29) Fried Apple Pies 92

(30) Quick and Easy Apple Delight 96

(31) Swedish Apple Pie 98

About the Author 100

Author's Afterthoughts 102

Delicious Apple Pie Recipes

MMMMMMMMMMMMMMMMMMMMMMMMMMMMMM

(1) Mom's Apple Pie

An apple pie cookbook wouldn't be complete without a traditional apple pie recipe passed down from generation to generation. I love serving this pie with some hot coffee and a large scoop of frozen yogurt or ice cream.

Total Prep Time: 30 minutes

Serving Size: 8

List of Ingredients:

- pastry for a 9" double crust pie
- 4 ounces butter, unsalted
- 1 ½ ounces all-purpose flour
- 2 ounces water
- 4 ounces white sugar
- 4 ounces brown sugar
- 8 peeled and cored green, sliced

MMMMMMMMMMMMMMMMMMMMMMMMMMMMMMMMMMM

Methods:

1. Preheat oven to 425 degrees Fahrenheit

2. Melt butter in a pan, then add flour and stir until paste-like in consistency

3. Mix in white and brown sugars and water and bring mixture to a boil

4. Reduce heat and let the sugar simmer

5. Arrange 1st crust in a 9" pie plate and place apples in the crust evenly

6. Take 2nd crust and cut into 1" strips and arrange in a lattice pattern over the apples

7. Pour the heated sugar over the top crust and bake for 15 minutes

8. Reduce heat to 350 degrees Fahrenheit for another 45 minutes or until apples are tender

(2) Cranberry Apple Pie

You would think the combination of cranberry and apple would produce a sour tasting pie, but this recipe proves that theory wrong. The combination of fruit and sugar creates the perfect tasting dessert that is not too sweet.

Total Prep Time: 20 minutes

Serving Size: 8

List of Ingredients:

- 2 x 9" prepared pie crusts
- 32 ounces cored and peeled apples, thinly sliced
- 16 ounces cranberries
- 6 ounces white sugar
- ½ ounce cornstarch
- 1 tsp. cinnamon, ground
- 1-ounce butter, cut into small pieces

MMMMMMMMMMMMMMMMMMMMMMMMMMMMMMMMMM

Methods:

1. Preheat oven to 400 degrees Fahrenheit

2. Spread crust over a 9" pie pan and pour apples into the bottom of the crust

3. Pour cranberries over the apples

4. Whisk sugar, cinnamon and cornstarch in a bowl and pour over the berries

5. Dot the top of the pie with pieces of butter and cover with the 2nd pie crust

6. Crimp the edges with your fingers or a fork and cut slits for steam

7. Bake for 1 hour or until golden brown

(3) Canadian Apple Pie

This pie recipe from my home country is chock full of juicy apples and fresh maple syrup. The combination of ingredients makes it a perfect dessert to serve with some dry white wine and a dollop of whip cream

Total Prep Time: 20 minutes

Serving Size: 8

List of Ingredients:

- pastry for a 9" double crust pie
- 1 ½ ounces cornstarch
- 1-ounce white sugar
- 1 tsp. cinnamon, ground
- 1 tsp. nutmeg, ground
- ¼ tsp. salt
- 40 ounces peeled and cored apples, thinly sliced
- 6 ounces pure maple syrup
- 1 egg
- 1 egg yolk
- ½ tsp. water

MMMMMMMMMMMMMMMMMMMMMMMMMMMMMMMMMM

Methods:

1. Preheat oven to 325 degrees Fahrenheit

2. Spread crust over a 9" pie plate

3. Combine sugar, cinnamon, cornstarch, nutmeg and salt in a bowl and whisk well

4. Mix in apples, whole egg and maple syrup and pour this mixture into the crust

5. Cover the filling with the 2nd crust and make slits in the top to allow for the escape of steam

6. Mix egg yolk and water together and brush this mixture over the top crust

7. Tent foil over the pie and bake for 35 minutes. Remove the foil and bake for another 15 minutes

(4) Easy Apple Pie

This recipe is simple to bake and tastes delicious warm or cold. I like to serve this with a generous scoop of ice cream or some chilled whipped topping.

Total Prep Time: 30 minutes

Serving Size: 8

List of Ingredients:

- 3 ounces butter, unsalted
- 2 ounces white sugar
- 4 ounces brown sugar
- 1 pinch salt
- ¼ tsp. cinnamon, ground
- 2 ounces water
- 15 ounces double crust prepared pie crust
- 4 peeled and cored red apples, sliced

MMMMMMMMMMMMMMMMMMMMMMMMMMMMMMMMM

Methods:

1. Preheat oven to 425 degrees Fahrenheit

2. Heat butter in a pan on medium heat, then stir in white and brown sugar, water and cinnamon. Stir until mixture has dissolved and bring to a boil

3. Remove pan from heat and set aside

4. Roll 1 pie crust into a 9" pie plate and press down to form a round shell

5. Arrange apple slices into the crust

6. On a flat surface dusted with flour, roll the second crust out and cut into 1" wide strips

7. Place the strips over the apples in a lattice pattern

8. Drizzle the heated syrup over the top crust

9. Bake for 15 minutes, then lower the heat to 350 degrees Fahrenheit and bake for another 40 minutes

(5) Caramel Pecan Apple Pie

This pie is a heavenly combination of crunchy, salty, sweet and creamy. It is everything you could want in a dessert and more. Serve with some maple ice cream and just a splash of caramel sauce to complete the experience.

Total Prep Time: 45 minutes

Serving Size: 8

List of Ingredients:

- 20 ounces all-purpose flour
- ½ tsp. salt
- 8 ounces chilled shortening
- 3 ounces ice water
- 4 ounces butter, unsalted
- 1 ½ ounces all-purpose flour
- 4 ounces white sugar
- 4 ounces packed brown sugar
- 2 ounces water
- 1/3 ounces vanilla extract
- 1 tsp. cinnamon, ground
- 1 pinch nutmeg, ground
- 2 ½ ounces butter
- 4 ounces packed brown sugar
- 8 ounces pecans, chopped
- 8 cored and peeled green apples, thinly sliced

MMMMMMMMMMMMMMMMMMMMMMMMMMMMMMMMMMM

Methods:

1. Whisk 20 ounces of flour and salt in a large bowl and add chilled shortening. Cut the shortening with a mixer until it is crumbly and resembles coarse meal

2. Add water a ½ ounce at a time. Mix with a fork as you add water and when you have a dough, roll together and shape into two separate balls

3. Wrap the dough in plastic and chill for 30 minutes

4. Preheat oven to 350 degrees Fahrenheit (175 degrees C).

5. Line a 9" pan with wax paper.

6. Melt 4 ounces of butter in a pan on medium heat

7. Add 1 ½ ounces of flour to the butter and stir until a paste is formed

8. Mix in 2 ounces of white sugar, 4 ounces brown sugar, 2 ounces water, cinnamon, vanilla, and nutmeg in the pan with the butter and bring to a boil. Reduce heat and simmer for 3 minutes or until thickened

9. Melt 2 ½ ounces of butter in another pan on low heat

10. Add 4 ounces of brown sugar to the butter and whisk until combined fully

11. Add pecans and stir well

12. Pour pecan mixture into the pie pan lined with wax paper

13. Mix apples and sugar, tossing until fruit is completely coated

14. Pour this mixture over the pecans, then spread the 2nd crust over the pie

15. Cut slits in the dough and tent foil over the pie

16. Bake for 1 hour

17. Put a plate over the top of the pie and flip it over. Remove the pie plate and wax paper and let cool for 1 hour

(6) Iron Skillet Apple Pie

When you bake the apple pie in a skillet, the taste is a combination of sweet and smoky. I will often make this dessert in the winter because I find it warms the belly on a cold day.

Total Prep Time: 30 minutes

Serving Size: 8

List of Ingredients:

- 4 ounces butter
- 8 ounces brown sugar
- 5 peeled and cored green apples, thinly sliced
- 3 x 9" refrigerated prepared pie crusts
- 8 ounces white sugar, divided
- 1/3 ounce cinnamon, divided
- 2 ounces white sugar
- ½ ounce chilled butter, cut into small pieces

MMMMMMMMMMMMMMMMMMMMMMMMMMMMMMMMMMMM

Methods:

1. Preheat oven to 350 degrees Fahrenheit

2. Place 4 ounces of butter in an oven-safe frying pan and place in the oven on low heat. When butter is melted, remove the frying pan from heat and sprinkle with brown sugar and place back in the oven to warm for 1 minute

3. Remove pan from the oven and arrange 1 pie crust in the frying pan to completely cover the brown sugar

4. Place sliced apples over the crust and top with 4 ounces of sugar and 1 tsp. of cinnamon

5. Place the second crust over the sugar and cinnamon and top that with the rest of the apple slices. Sprinkle with the rest of the sugar and add the butter pieces

6. Cut slits into the top of the pie to allow for the escape of steam

7. Bake for 45 minutes or until apples are tender

(7) Mini Apple Pies with Almonds

These adorable miniature pies are the perfect size for a lunchtime snack at work or to pack in the kids' lunches. You can dress them up by piping rosettes of whipped topping before serving.

Total Prep Time: 25 minutes

Serving Size: 18

List of Ingredients:

- 4 ounces packed brown sugar, divided
- 2 ½ ounces almonds, sliced
- 2 ounces all-purpose flour
- 1 ½ ounces cold butter
- Cooking spray
- 15 ounces refrigerated pie crusts
- 16 ounces cored and peeled apples, chopped
- ½ tsp. cinnamon, ground
- ½ tsp. vanilla extract
- Thawed frozen whipped topping

MMMMMMMMMMMMMMMMMMMMMMMMMMMMMMMMMM

Methods:

1. Preheat oven to 375 degrees Fahrenheit

2. Mix 3 ounces of brown sugar, almonds and flour in a bowl and cut in butter with a mixer until the consistency is mealy

3. Coat an 18 muffin cup tin with cooking spray

4. Roll pie crust onto a flat surface dusted with flour. Cut into 9 equal squares and press into the muffin cups

5. Mix apples, 1 ounce of brown sugar, cinnamon and vanilla and scoop 2 ounces of the apple mix into the cups

6. Bake for 20 minutes, remove from heat and sprinkle with the crumble. Bake for another 10 minutes

7. Add a dollop of whipped topping before serving

(8) Caramel Apple Pie

If you love caramel apples, then you will go crazy for this recipe. The combination of tastes makes this pie addictive and filling.

Total Prep Time: 30 minutes

Serving Size: 8

List of Ingredients:

- Pastry for a 9" refrigerated pie crusts
- 8 ounces granulated sugar
- 2 ounces all-purpose flour
- 1 tsp. cinnamon, ground
- 40 ounces peeled and cored apples, thinly sliced
- 4 ounces caramel apple dip
- 1 ounce milk
- 8 ounces all-purpose flour
- 4 ounces packed brown sugar
- 4 ounces butter

MMMMMMMMMMMMMMMMMMMMMMMMMMMMMMMMMMM

Methods:

Heat oven to 375°Fahrenheit

Make the pie crusts according to the instructions on the package and allow to cool

Mix granulated sugar, 2 ounces of flour and cinnamon in a large bowl

Toss apples in the flour mixture until thoroughly coated

Transfer coated apples into the 1st crust.

Mix 1 ounce of the caramel dip and milk and drizzle this mixture over the apples

Mix 8 ounces of flour and brown sugar in a large bowl and blend butter into the mixture with an electric mixer until it resembles coarse oatmeal

Place 2nd crust on a flat surface and cut 1" strips

Arrange strips in a lattice pattern over the apples in the 1st crust and pinch around the edge to create a finished look

Bake for 60 minutes or until apples are tender and crust is golden brown

Drizzle the rest of the caramel dip over the top after it has cooled for a few minutes and set aside for 2 hours

(9) Dutch Apple Berry Pie

This refreshing pie tastes lovely with some frozen yogurt or whipped topping. Try sprinkling some cinnamon over the top to enhance the flavor of the fresh fruit.

Total Prep Time: 20 minutes

Serving Size: 8

List of Ingredients:

- 16 ounces green apples, sliced
- 4 ounces raspberries
- 4 ounces fresh blueberries
- 9" deep dish pie crust
- 5 ½ ounces all-purpose flour
- 5 ½ ounces packed brown sugar
- 2 ½ ounces butter
- ½ tsp. cinnamon, ground
- ½ tsp. allspice, ground
- 1 pinch nutmeg, ground

MMMMMMMMMMMMMMMMMMMMMMMMMMMMMMMMM

Methods:

1. Preheat oven to 350 degrees Fahrenheit

2. Combine berries and apples thoroughly and pour fruit into the pie crust

3. Mix the rest of the ingredients in a bowl until fully combined and pour over the filling in the crust

4. Bake for 30 minutes or until brown and bubbling

(10) Mini Apple Pies

These divine miniature pies are a perfect dish to make for a pot-luck or outdoor barbecue with the family. These individual-sized treats also freeze well, so you can make extra and have some for snacking.

Total Prep Time: 20 minutes

Serving Size: 4

List of Ingredients:

- 2 x 9" single crust pie pastries
- 24 ounces green apples, diced
- 1-ounce instant tapioca
- 4 ounces white sugar
- lemon juice
- 1/8 tsp. nutmeg, ground
- ¼ tsp. cinnamon, ground

MMMMMMMMMMMMMMMMMMMMMMMMMMMMMMMM

Methods:

1. Preheat oven to 400 degrees Fahrenheit

2. Roll pie crust out on a flat surface dusted with flour

3. With a 6" round cookie cutter, cut 4 circles out of the pie crusts and stretch them out onto small pie dishes of 5" each

4. Cut the rest of the dough into small strips to fit over the filling

5. Mix apple, sugar, lemon juice, cinnamon, nutmeg and tapioca together in a large bowl and set aside for 5 minutes to soften

6. Stir mixture thoroughly and dole out into the individual pie shells with a spoon

7. Create lattice patterns over the mini apple pies with the cut crust and pinch along the edges to close the dough

8. Bake for 30 minutes or until the crust becomes golden brown and apples are bubbling

(11) Apple Pizza Pie

This pie is fun to eat and is a perfect treat for a kids' birthday party and even a special weekend breakfast. If you want to jazz it up a bit, try sprinkling this pizza with some fresh berries or preserves.

Total Prep Time: 30 minutes

Serving Size: 8

List of Ingredients:

- 4 ounces softened butter
- 2 ounces confectioners' sugar
- 8 ounces all-purpose flour, sifted
- 42 ounces apple pie filling
- 8 ounces Cheddar cheese, shredded
- 6 ounces all-purpose flour
- 4 ounces packed brown sugar
- ½ tsp. cinnamon, ground

MMMMMMMMMMMMMMMMMMMMMMMMMMMMMMMMMM

Methods:

1. Preheat oven to 350 degrees Fahrenheit.

2. Combine butter and confectioners' sugar together with a mixer until creamy

3. Add 8 ounces of flour and slowly mix until consistency is that of dough

4. Spread dough out onto a pizza pan of 12"

5. Bake for 15 minutes

6. Remove from heat, spread the apple filling evenly over the dough

7. Mix the rest of the ingredients together and sprinkle over the apple pie filling

8. Bake for 30 minutes or until the edges of crust turn golden brown

(12) Extra Spicy Apple Pie

Kick up the spice a little when you make this saucy dessert. If you aren't sure how much spice you like, then try using less than is required and perform taste tests to check.

Total Prep Time: 30 minutes

Serving Size: 8

List of Ingredients:

- 9" double crust pie pastry
- 32 ounces peeled and cored green apples, chopped
- 8 ounces white sugar
- 8 ounces light brown sugar
- 1 ounces all-purpose flour
- ½ tsp. cinnamon, ground
- 1/8 tsp. nutmeg, ground
- ¼ tsp. coriander, ground
- ¼ tsp. allspice, ground
- 1/8 tsp. cloves, ground
- ½ ounce softened butter
- ½ ounce turbinado sugar

MMMMMMMMMMMMMMMMMMMMMMMMMMMMMMMMM

Methods:

1. Preheat oven to 350 degrees Fahrenheit

2. Roll out dough for both crusts, placing 1st crust onto a 9" pie plate and the second set aside

3. Mix apples, white and brown sugar, 1 ounce of flour, coriander, nutmeg, cloves and allspice in a large bowl and pour this mixture in the pie shell

4. Arrange butter pieces around the filling and cover with the 2nd crust, pressing the edges with your fingers to crimp

5. Make small slits in the top and sprinkle the turbinado over the top evenly

6. Bake for 90 minutes or until the crust is golden brown and the filling is done

(13) Upside Down Apple Pecan Pie

This funny looking pie is the most delicious upside-down pie I have ever tasted, and I always get rave reviews. Serve this warm with some ice cream or frozen yogurt as a special dessert treat.

Total Prep Time: 30 minutes

Serving Size: 8

List of Ingredients:

- 1 cup chopped pecans
- 1/3 cup margarine, melted
- ½ cup firmly packed brown sugar
- 6 cups Granny Smith apples – cored, peeled and sliced
- 1 pastry for a 9 inch double crust pie
- 2 Tbsp. all-purpose flour
- ¼ cup white sugar
- 1/8 tsp. ground nutmeg
- ½ tsp. ground cinnamon

MMMMMMMMMMMMMMMMMMMMMMMMMMMMMMMMMMMM

Methods:

1. Preheat oven to 375 degrees Fahrenheit.

2. Mix brown sugar, pecans and margarine in a bowl and spread evenly in a 9" deep-dish pan

3. Roll crust onto the pecan mixture and press down to firmly secure

4. Combine apple slices, flour, cinnamon, sugar and nutmeg in a large bowl and pour into the pie pan

5. Place 2nd crust over the apples and crimp with your fingers along the edges

6. Make small slits in the top of the crust

7. Tent foil over the pie and bake for 50 minutes or until golden brown

8. Remove pie and let it cool

9. Place plate over the top of the pie and flip over

10. Allow to cool before removing the pan

11. Cool for 2 hours before serving

(14) Sour Cream Apple Pie

The sour cream in this recipe gives this dish a unique tart taste that I find a refreshing change to the sweet variety. Try serving this with a light wine to complement the flavor.

Total Prep Time: 20 minutes

Serving Size: 8

List of Ingredients:

- 9" pie crust, unbaked
- 6 ounces sugar
- 1-ounce all-purpose flour
- 1/8 tsp. salt
- 8 ounces sour cream
- ½ tsp. vanilla extract
- 1 egg
- 16 ounces apples, diced
- 2 ½ ounces sugar
- 2 ½ ounces all-purpose flour
- 1 tsp. cinnamon, ground
- 2 ounces butter, chilled and diced

MMMMMMMMMMMMMMMMMMMMMMMMMMMMMMMM

Methods:

1. Preheat the oven to 425 degrees Fahrenheit

2. Press the crust into a 9" pie plate evenly

3. Stir 6 ounces of sugar, salt and 1 ounce of flour in a bowl until combined well

4. Add sour cream, vanilla and egg and mix with an electric mixer until smooth

5. Mix in apples until coated thoroughly

6. Pour the apple filling into the pie crust and bake for 15 minutes

7. Reduce heat to 350 degrees Fahrenheit and bake for another 30 minutes

8. Stir in 2 ½ ounces of flour, 2 ½ ounces of sugar and cinnamon in a bowl, then mix in butter until the mixture looks like crumbs

9. Remove pie from the oven, cover the top with the crumb mixture, then place in the oven for another 15 minutes

10. Chill pie before serving

(15) Apple Sheet Cake

The frosting on this cake is sweet and delicious, and I usually don't find the need for ice cream or whipped topping to complete this pie. Try a beverage for a pairing that has little sugar, so you don't overwhelm your taste buds.

Total Prep Time: 30 minutes

Serving Size: 25

List of Ingredients:

- 24 ounces all-purpose flour
- 1 ½ tsp. baking powder
- 1 tsp. salt
- 4 ounces shortening
- 8 ounces milk
- 48 ounces peeled and cored apples, thinly sliced
- 8 ounces white sugar
- 1 tsp. cinnamon, ground
- 1 ounce all-purpose flour
- 4 ounces butter
- 20 ounces confectioners' sugar
- 1 ½ ounces milk
- 2 ½ ounces softened butter
- ½ tsp. vanilla extract

MMMMMMMMMMMMMMMMMMMMMMMMMMMMMMMM

Methods:

1. Mix 24 ounces of flour, baking powder and salt in a bowl until combined thoroughly

2. Cut shortening into the flour mixture until the consistency is mealy

3. Slowly add 8 ounces of milk to the meal and stir until well combined

4. Roll into two even dough balls, cover with plastic wrap and chill for 30 minutes

5. Preheat oven to 400 degrees Fahrenheit

6. Roll dough balls onto a flat surface dusted with flour and spread the first one out onto a 10"x15" pie pan, allowing extra dough to fall over the edge

7. Add apples, cinnamon, sugar and 1 ounce of flour in a bowl and toss until fruit is completely coated

8. Pour into the pie pan

9. Slice 4 ounces of butter and dot the filling

10. Place the 2nd crust over the apples and crimp edges with your fingers or a fork

11. Cut slits in the top

12. Bake for 30 minutes, remove from heat and let cool for 10 minutes

13. Beat confectioners' sugar, 1 ½ ounces of milk, 2 ½ ounces of butter and vanilla until creamy

14. Spread over the pie evenly and serve

(16) Apple Blueberry Pie

Nothing tastes quite like the combination of apples and blueberries when mixed in this delicious pie. Serve this with some sweet wine to complement the tangy flavor of the fruit.

Total Prep Time: 20 minutes

Serving Size: 8

List of Ingredients:

- 24 ounces cored and peeled apples, sliced
- 8 ounces blueberries
- 9" unbaked deep-dish pie crust
- ¼ tsp. salt
- 2 ounces all-purpose flour
- 4 ounces white sugar
- ¼ tsp. nutmeg, ground
- ¼ tsp. cinnamon, ground
- 8 ounces plain yogurt
- 1 egg
- 1 tsp. vanilla extract
- 4 ounces all-purpose flour
- 4 ounces pecans, chopped
- 4 ounces rolled oats
- 2 ounces brown sugar
- 4 ounces butter

MMMMMMMMMMMMMMMMMMMMMMMMMMMMMMMMMMM

Methods:

1. Preheat oven to 400 Fahrenheit

2. Arrange apples and berries into the pie crust

3. Combine 2 ounces flour, white sugar, nutmeg, salt and cinnamon in a bowl

4. Mix in egg, vanilla and yogurt, then pour the mixture over the fruit in the crust

5. Combine 4 ounces flour, oats, pecans and brown sugar, then cut butter into the mixture until it resembles coarse meal

6. Bake pie for 15 minutes, then reduce heat to 350 degrees Fahrenheit and bake for another 30 minutes

7. Spread crumble over the pie and bake for 15 minutes

(17) French Apple Pie with Cream Cheese Topping

The topping on this pie is creamy, rich and decadent and makes this apple pie an addictive dessert. Try this with some mint tea or flavored coffee as a complement to the taste of the cream cheese.

Total Prep Time: 20 minutes

Serving Size: 8

List of Ingredients:

- 2 ounces softened butter
- 8 ounces white sugar
- 1 egg
- ¼ tsp. salt
- 1 tsp. cinnamon, ground
- 1 tsp. nutmeg, ground
- 1 tsp. baking soda
- 8 ounces all-purpose flour
- 4 ounces walnuts, chopped
- 20 ounces cored and peeled apples, diced
- 1 tsp. vanilla extract
- 1 ounce hot water
- 3 ounces softened cream cheese
- 1 ½ ounces softened unsalted butter
- ½ tsp. vanilla extract
- 12 ounces confectioners' sugar, sifted

MMMMMMMMMMMMMMMMMMMMMMMMMMMMMMMMM

Methods:

1. Preheat the oven to 350 degrees Fahrenheit

2. Coat a 9" pie pan with cooking oil

3. Mix 2 ounces of white sugar, butter, salt, cinnamon, egg, soda, nutmeg, flour 1 tsp. of vanilla, apples and hot water in a bowl

4. Mix until thickened

5. Pour the filling into the pie pan

6. Bake for 45 minutes

7. Let cool before adding the frosting

8. Mix cream cheese, 1 ½ ounces of butter, the rest of the vanilla, and confectioners' sugar in a bowl and beat until smooth

9. Spread over the cooled pie

(18) Blueberry Apple Peach Pie

The triple threat of fruit in this recipe create a unique and scrumptious flavor when you take your first bite. Try serving this pie with some dry white wine or red wine to enhance the taste of the ingredients.

Total Prep Time: 40 minutes

Serving Size: 8

List of Ingredients:

- 9" double crust deep dish pie pastry
- 48 ounces cored and peeled apples, sliced thinly
- 24 ounces peeled and cored peaches, thinly sliced
- ½ ounces fresh lemon juice
- 2 ounces granulated sugar
- 4 ounces pie filling thickener
- ½ ounce cornstarch
- ½ tsp. salt
- ½ tsp. cinnamon, ground
- 8 ounces fresh blueberries
- ½ tsp. vanilla
- 8 ounces all-purpose flour
- 5 ½ ounces packed brown sugar
- 4 ounces old-fashioned oats
- ½ tsp. cinnamon, ground
- ¼ tsp. salt
- 4 ounces chilled unsalted butter
- ½ tsp. milk
- Coarse sugar for topping

MMMMMMMMMMMMMMMMMMMMMMMMMMMMMMMMMM

Methods:

Heat oven to 400°Fahrenheit

Prepare pie crusts according to instructions on package

Combine peaches and apples in a bowl and sprinkle lemon juice over the fruit

Mix 6 ounces of granulated sugar, filling thickener, cornstarch, ½ tsp. of salt and ½ tsp. of cinnamon in a bowl and pour over the apples and peaches. Toss the fruit to make sure it is thoroughly coated

Stir in blueberries and vanilla gently, then pour the filling into the pie plate

Combine flour, 5 ½ ounces of brown sugar, 4 ounces of oats, ½ tsp. of cinnamon and ¼ ounce of salt in a bowl, then cut the chilled unsalted butter into the mixture until it is the consistency of coarse meal

Sprinkle the crumble over the filling in the pie

Roll the 2nd crust on a flat surface dusted with flour, then cut into 1" strips

Arrange the strips over the filling in a lattice pattern and crimp edges with your fingers or a fork

Mix milk and coarse sugar in a bowl and brush over the top crust

Tent foil over the pie and bake for 30 minutes. Remove the foil and bake for another 40 minutes or until it turns golden brown

Cool for a few hours before serving

(19) Apple Buttermilk Custard Pie

This creamy custard pie is a different apple pie that is a lovely complement to a light dinner. Pair a robust red wine with this dish to accentuate the taste of the custard.

Total Prep Time: 15 minutes

Serving Size: 8

List of Ingredients:

- 9" pie shell
- 2 ounces butter
- 2 cored and peeled tart apples, thinly sliced
- 4 ounces white sugar
- ½ tsp. cinnamon, ground
- 2 ounces softened butter
- 10 ½ ounces white sugar
- 4 eggs
- 1 tsp. vanilla extract
- 1-ounce all-purpose flour
- 6 ounces buttermilk
- 2 ounces white sugar
- 2 ounces packed brown sugar
- 4 ounces all-purpose flour
- ¼ tsp. cinnamon, ground
- 1 ½ ounces butter

MMMMMMMMMMMMMMMMMMMMMMMMMMMMMMMMMMMM

Methods:

1. Preheat oven to 300 degrees Fahrenheit.

2. Melt 2 ounces of butter in a frying pan on medium heat

3. Stir in apple slices, 4 ounces of white sugar and ½ tsp. of cinnamon for 5 minutes or until apples are soft

4. Combine 2 ounces of butter and 10 ½ ounces of white sugar in a bowl and beat until smooth

5. Add eggs to the butter and sugar one at a time and beat until combined completely

6. Stir in vanilla and buttermilk. Beat mixture until creamy

7. Spread pastry over the pie pan, making a couple of holes with a fork

8. Pour the apple filling into the crust and pour the buttermilk mixture over the apples

9. Bake for 30 minutes

10. Mix 2 ounces of white sugar, brown sugar, 4 ounces of flour and ¼ tsp. of a cinnamon in a bowl. Add butter and cut until it is the consistency of coarse meal

11. Remove pie from heat and arrange crumble over the pie evenly. Bake for another 50 minutes or until it is cooked enough for a knife to be inserted and removed without filling on it

12. Leave for 1 hour before serving

(20) Apple Pockets

My kids love these tasty treats, and they fit nicely into lunch bags for school. You can make a whole bunch of the pockets and freeze them as well for snacks.

Total Prep Time: 20 minutes

Serving Size: 6

List of Ingredients:

- 3 peeled and cored sweet apples, sliced thinly
- 1 ounce sugar
- 1 ounce flour
- 1 pinch of salt
- 1 tsp. apple pie spice
- ½ ounce vanilla extract
- 15 ounce thawed unbaked pie crust, thawed
- milk
- 1 beaten egg

MMMMMMMMMMMMMMMMMMMMMMMMMMMMMMMMMMM

Methods:

1. Preheat oven to 375 degrees Fahrenheit

2. Mix flour, spice, salt and vanilla in a bowl, then toss apples until fully coated

3. Coat a baking sheet with cooking spray and roll the dough out, pressing down with your fingers until flat

4. Place apple mixture onto one part of the dough and leave a small border of 1"

5. Brush the dough with milk and fold the dough over carefully

6. Create a pocket shape and pinch the edges to close

7. Cut slits in the top of the dough pocket and brush with egg

8. Bake for 40 minutes or until golden brown

(21) Autumn Fruit Tart

This pie is perfect for any meal of the day, even as a breakfast treat. The juicy apple flavor goes well with a morning coffee or an aperitif at the end of the evening.

Total Prep Time: 15 minutes

Serving Size: 8

List of Ingredients:

- 4 ounces cream cheese
- 12 ounces all-purpose flour
- 2 cored and peeled apples, thinly sliced
- 1 cored and peeled pear, thinly sliced
- 2 ounces orange juice
- 2 ½ ounces brown sugar
- ½ tsp. cinnamon, ground
- ¼ tsp. cardamom, ground
- ¼ tsp. nutmeg, ground
- ¾ ounce cornstarch
- 4 ounce warm apricot jam

MMMMMMMMMMMMMMMMMMMMMMMMMMMMMMMMMM

Methods:

1. Combine butter and cream cheese with flour in a large bowl and cut with a mixer or a knife until the consistency is that of coarse meal

2. Roll the mixture into a ball and chill for 2 hours

3. Mix apples and pears with orange juice in a separate bowl

4. Whisk cinnamon, nutmeg, brown sugar, cardamom and cornstarch together until combined well

5. Add apples and pears and toss until fruit is thoroughly coated

6. Preheat oven to 375 degrees Fahrenheit

7. Coat a tart pan of 8" with cooking spray

8. Roll chilled dough onto a flat surface dusted with flour and cut out 10" circles in the dough

9. Spread the cut dough on the tart pan

10. Pour the fruit filling into the dough and fold the extra dough over the fruit

11. Bake for 30 minutes or until filling is bubbly

12. Remove from the oven and brush with the apricot jam

(22) Apple Crumble Pie

This crumble was the very first apple pie recipe I ever tried, and I must say, it was sensational! I made this for a baking competition and came in first place.

Total Prep Time: 30 minutes

Serving Size: 8

List of Ingredients:

- 9" deep dish pie crust
- 40 ounces peeled and cored green apples, sliced thinly
- 4 ounces white sugar
- ¾ tsp. cinnamon, ground
- 2 ½ ounces white sugar
- 6 ounces all-purpose flour
- 3 ounces butter

MMMMMMMMMMMMMMMMMMMMMMMMMMMMMMMMM

Methods:

1. Preheat oven to 400 degrees Fahrenheit

2. Place pie shell in a 9" pie plate, then place apples in the crust

3. Mix 4 ounces of sugar and cinnamon and pour over the apples

4. Mix 2 ½ ounces of sugar and flour in a bowl and mix the butter in, cutting it into the mixture until it becomes crumbly

5. Spread this crumble over the apples evenly and bake for about 40 minutes or until apples are tender

(23) Apple Berry Pie

The combination of fruit in this recipe has the perfect amount of tart and sweet tastes. I would serve this pie with a sweet wine or fruity tea to complement the flavor of the berries.

Total Prep Time: 20 minutes

Serving Size: 8

List of Ingredients:

- 9 " double crust pie pastry
- 8 ounces white sugar
- 2/3 ounce tapioca
- ½ tsp. cinnamon, ground
- 16 ounces fresh blackberries
- 16 ounces peeled and cored apples, sliced thinly
- 1 ounce butter, cut into small pieces

MMMMMMMMMMMMMMMMMMMMMMMMMMMMMMMMMMM

Methods:

1. Preheat oven to 375 degrees Fahrenheit

2. Roll crust out onto a flat surface dusted with flour and place one in a 9" pie plate and set the 2nd one aside

3. Mix sugar, cinnamon and tapioca in a bowl, then add apples and berries. Toss mixture until fruit is coated thoroughly. Let stand for 30 minutes.

4. Pour filling into the pie plate and arrange butter pieces evenly over the filling

5. Cover with the 2nd crust and crimp along the edges

6. Cut slits in the top of the crust and tent foil over the pie

7. Bake for 25 minutes, remove the foil, then bake for another 20 minutes or until golden brown

(24) Delicious Caramel Apple Pie

This entry is the second caramel apple pie recipes in this book, and equally as delicious. If you are in the mood for something stronger than wine, then a malt whiskey tastes superb with this dessert.

Total Prep Time: 30 minutes

Serving Size: 8

List of Ingredients:

- Pastry for a 9" double crust deep dish pie
- 4 ounces brown sugar
- 2 ounces melted butter
- 2 ½ ounces all-purpose flour
- 40 ounces apples, sliced thinly
- 5 ½ ounces white sugar
- 1 ½ ounces all-purpose flour
- 1/3 ounce cinnamon, ground
- 1 tsp. lemon juice
- 20 caramels, halved
- 1 ounce milk

MMMMMMMMMMMMMMMMMMMMMMMMMMMMMMMM

Methods:

1. Preheat the oven to 375 degrees Fahrenheit

2. Mix brown sugar, butter and 2 ½ ounces of flour in a bowl and then set aside

3. Put apples, white sugar, 1 ½ ounces of flour, lemon juice and cinnamon in a bowl and toss until apples are thoroughly coated

4. Place dough into a deep dish pie plate and pour half of the apple mixture over the pastry

5. Cover with 10 of the caramels and half of the brown sugar mixture

6. Arrange the 2nd crust over the apple filling and press with your fingers to create crimps around the edges

7. Cut slits in the top of the crust

8. Tent foil over the pie and place on baking sheet

9. Bake for 25 minutes or until the crust is golden brown

(25) Sugar-Free Apple Pie

If you are looking for an apple pie with all-natural ingredients and sweetened without preservatives or chemicals, then this recipe is for you. I would serve this with your favorite herbal tea or fruit-infused water.

Total Prep Time: 30 minutes

Serving Size: 8

List of Ingredients:

- 2 x 9" prepared pie shells
- 1 ½ ounces cornstarch
- ½ ounce cinnamon, ground
- 12 ounces thawed frozen apple juice concentrate, unsweetened
- 48 ounces green apples, sliced

MMMMMMMMMMMMMMMMMMMMMMMMMMMMMMMMM

Methods:

1. Preheat the oven to 350 degrees Fahrenheit

2. Whisk cinnamon, cornstarch and 2 ½ ounces of concentrate in a bowl and set aside

3. Place apples in a saucepan with the rest of the juice concentrate and cook on medium heat for about 10 minutes or until apples are soft

4. Add cornstarch mix to the saucepan and cook for another 5-10 minutes or until thick

5. Remove the saucepan from heat and pour the filling into the 1st pie crust

6. Place the 2nd pie crust onto the apple filling and crimp with your fingers to close the edges

7. Cut slits in the top of the crust and bake for 45 minutes or until golden brown

(26) Glazed Apple Cream Pie

This pie is sweet, creamy and decadent so it probably won't last long when served. Try serving this with a dry wine, so you don't overload on sugary tastes or a mild tea.

Total Prep Time: 15 minutes

Serving Size: 8

List of Ingredients:

- 4 ounces white sugar
- 4 ounces milk
- 4 ounces heavy cream
- 2 ounces butter
- 1 ounce cornstarch
- 1 ounce milk
- 1 tsp. vanilla extract
- 2 peeled and cored tart apples, sliced
- ½ ounce all-purpose flour
- ¼ tsp. cinnamon, ground
- 15 ounce package pastry for double-crust pie
- 4 ounces confectioners' sugar
- ½ ounce milk
- ¼ tsp. vanilla extract
- ½ ounce softened butter

MMMMMMMMMMMMMMMMMMMMMMMMMMMMMMMM

Methods:

1. Preheat oven to 400 degrees Fahrenheit

2. Heat 4 ounces of sugar, 4 ounces of milk, 4 ounces of cream and 2 ounces of butter in a large pan on medium heat

3. Stir mixture until butter is melted and the ingredients are well combined

4. Whisk 1 ounce of milk, cornstarch and vanilla in a bowl and add to the pan

5. Cook for 5 minutes or until thick

6. Remove from heat and set aside to cool

7. Cook until thickened, stirring constantly. Remove from heat, and set aside to cool slightly.

8. Mix apples, cinnamon and flour in a large bowl

9. Arrange dough in a 9" pie plate and pour the cooled mixture in the pan into the crust, then place apples over the top

10. Place 2nd crust on the apples, cut slits in the crust in and bake for 40 minutes or until the apples are tender and the crust is golden brown

11. Mix the rest of the ingredients in a bowl and pour over the baked pie. Chill for 2 hours before serving

(27) Apple Crumb Pie

My family loves the topping on this apple pie, and comments that they could eat it alone without any of the fillings, it is so good. Serve this delectable treat with some vanilla ice cream and a lovely glass of white wine for a special dessert.

Total Prep Time: 30 minutes

Serving Size: 8

List of Ingredients:

- 9" prepared pie shell
- 48 ounces apples, thinly sliced
- ½ ounce lemon juice
- 6 ounces white sugar
- 1 ounce all-purpose flour
- ½ tsp. cinnamon, ground
- 1/8 tsp. nutmeg, ground
- 4 ounces raisins
- 4 ounces walnuts, chopped
- 4 ounces all-purpose flour
- 4 ounces brown sugar
- 1 ½ ounces butter

MMMMMMMMMMMMMMMMMMMMMMMMMMMMMMMMM

Methods:

1. Preheat oven to 375 degrees Fahrenheit

2. Sprinkle lemon juice over apple slices in a bowl, then mix in white sugar, 1 ounces of flour, nutmeg and cinnamon. Mix together until apples are thoroughly coated, then add raisins and walnuts

3. Pour apples into the pie shell

4. Mix 4 ounces of flour and brown sugar in a bowl, then add butter. Cut the mixture until it resembles a crumble and spread over the apples in the pie shell

5. Tent foil over the pie and bake for 25 minutes.

6. Remove foil from the pie and bake for another 30 minutes or until crust is golden brown

(28) Fried Apple Pies

This apple pie recipe reminds of state fairs and carnivals I used to frequent as a kid. These fried treats hit the spot after a day of playing in the snow in the winter.

Total Prep Time: 45 minutes

Serving Size: 8

List of Ingredients:

For the Pastry:

- 16 ounces all-purpose flour
- 4 ounces chilled shortening
- 1 tsp. salt
- 4 ounces cold water

For the Apple Filling:

- 2 peeled and cored apples, diced
- 2 ounces white sugar
- 1/8 tsp. cinnamon, ground
- Cooking oil

MMMMMMMMMMMMMMMMMMMMMMMMMMMMMMMMMMM

Methods:

1. Place flour and salt in a bowl and sift together

2. Add shortening to the bowl and cut until the consistency is crumbly

3. Add cold water ½ ounce at a time slowly to the shortening and mix in between

4. When you have a dough in the bowl, roll it up and place it in plastic wrap. Chill for 1 hour

5. Mix sugar and cinnamon into a small bowl and set aside

6. Place diced apples into a saucepan and pour the sugar and cinnamon over top

7. Toss mixture until apples are thoroughly coated

8. Cover the saucepan and cook on low heat until apples are soft

9. Crush the apples until the consistency is that of a thick sauce

10. Roll chilled dough out onto a flat surface dusted with flour until it is 1/8" thick

11. Cut small circles into the dough with 4" round cookie cutters

12. Spoon filling onto one side of each round, fold the dough over and then crimp the edges using a fork to close the dough

13. Heat oil in a large pan at 375 degrees Fahrenheit and fry the pies 2-3 at a time, cooking each side for 3 minutes or until golden brown

(29) Quick and Easy Apple Delight

This recipe is fun to make and eat, especially when it is warmed up and served with a chilled whipped topping. I have served this in champagne glasses with a dollop of ice cream for added effect at parties.

Total Prep Time: 5 minutes

Serving Size: 12

List of Ingredients:

- 42 ounces apple pie filling
- 18 ¼ ounces yellow cake mix
- 4 ounces melted butter

MMMMMMMMMMMMMMMMMMMMMMMMMMMMMMMMMMM

Methods:

1. Preheat oven to 350 degrees Fahrenheit

2. Pour the filling into a pie plate measuring 9"x13"

3. Sprinkle yellow cake mix on the pie filling

4. Pour the butter onto the top of the cake mix and bake for 30 minutes

(30) Swedish Apple Pie

The Swedes know how to make a delicious apple pie without too much effort on the chef's part. Try this treat with some flavored coffee or mint tea.

Total Prep Time: 20 minutes

Serving Size: 8

List of Ingredients:

- 24 ounces peeled and cored green apples, sliced
- ½ ounce sugar
- 8 ounces sugar
- 8 ounces flour
- 1 tsp. cinnamon
- 6 ounces butter, melted
- 1 egg

MMMMMMMMMMMMMMMMMMMMMMMMMMMMMMMMMMMM

Methods:

1. Preheat oven to 350 degrees Fahrenheit

2. Place ½ ounce of sugar in a bowl and toss apples in the sugar until thoroughly coated. Pour the apples into a 9" pie plate

3. Mix 4 ounces of sugar, flour, butter, egg and cinnamon together, then spread evenly over the apples

4. Bake for 45 minutes or until golden brown

About the Author

A native of Indianapolis, Indiana, Valeria Ray found her passion for cooking while she was studying English Literature at Oakland City University. She decided to try a cooking course with her friends and the experience changed her forever. She enrolled at the Art Institute of Indiana which offered extensive courses in the culinary Arts. Once Ray dipped her toe in the cooking world, she never looked back.

When Valeria graduated, she worked in French restaurants in the Indianapolis area until she became the head chef at one of the 5-star establishments in the area. Valeria's attention to taste and visual detail caught the eye of a local business person who expressed an interest in publishing her recipes. Valeria began her secondary career authoring cookbooks and e-books which she tackled with as much talent and gusto as her first career. Her passion for food leaps off the page of her books which have colourful anecdotes and stunning pictures of dishes she has prepared herself.

Valeria Ray lives in Indianapolis with her husband of 15 years, Tom, her daughter, Isobel and their loveable Golden Retriever, Goldy. Valeria enjoys cooking special dishes in her large, comfortable kitchen where the family gets involved in preparing meals. This successful, dynamic chef is an inspiration to culinary students and novice cooks everywhere.

Author's Afterthoughts

Thank you for Purchasing my book and taking the time to read it from front to back. I am always grateful when a reader chooses my work and I hope you enjoyed it!

With the vast selection available online, I am touched that you chose to be purchasing my work and take valuable time out of your life to read it. My hope is that you feel you made the right decision.

I very much would like to know what you thought of the book. Please take the time to write an honest and informative review on Amazon.com. Your experience and opinions will be of great benefit to me and those readers looking to make an informed choice.

With much thanks,

Valeria Ray

Printed in Dunstable, United Kingdom